Latest best job interview tips that'll amaze interviewers

Mac Nekzy

DISCLAIMER

This ebook has been written for information purposes whereby it's made with the effort and possibly to provide basic informations and also guide youths through the difficult job interviews that they might have been finding difficult to secure their dream jobs.

The purpose of this ebook is to educate and the author and the publisher shall neither liability nor responsible to per-person or entity with respect to any loss or damage caused or alleged to be caused directly or indirectly by this book.

DEDICATION

This job interview guide manual is dedicated to my family who supported me from the very start,also to my friends and well wishers.

ACKNOWLEDGMENTS

First kudos to the Almighty God for the wisdom,His love and mercy towards me.Gratitude goes to those who believe in me,those who supported me both family and friends,I appreciate and thank you all.

CONTENTS

INTRODUCTION

If not longer now everybody will truly undergo or revel in the horrible,terrifying and intimidating mission of interviewing for a process.Even if its for simply any process to live on with or to maintain your payments paid, or if its the dream process youve constantly dreamt approximately,earlier than you could get that process which you definitely choice there are such a lot of matters that you need to recall additionally installed act or in movement earlier than you could get that your dream process.Most human beings anticipate to end that the maximum crucial a part of a process interview is displaying up neat, nicely groomed,searching appropriate and all that however there's greater to it than all that.

All the matters that you may ever want to steady the process can be on the way you behave, give yourself and convince yourself why you're in an appropriate role to steady the process. The tiniest aspect can suggest the distinction among your having a new process, or youre nevertheless pounding the pavement seeking to steady a brand new interview.It is not unusual place know-how that it's miles commonly the smallest element that reasons human beings to fail a process interview. The reality that you could steadily rating an interview in any respect proves that you have already got the proper know-how or thoughts for the process.So however, scoring the interview is simply step one in the adventure this is to get you the process of your dreams.This ebook I wrote is to be your complete manual to triumphing and securing that your dream job.Below are the indexed steps that you should recognize approximately to get you via the process interview.In this ebook I wrote, you'll learn:

1.How to get the interview of your choice.

2.How to put it together for the interview.

3.How to make a first rate first impression.

4.How to behave yourself at some stage in the interview.

5.What the maximum not unusual place questions are.

6.What inquiries to ask your interviewer.

7.What not unusual place errors you have to keep away from making.

8.About the submit interview observe-up.

9.Questions that interviewers can't ask

CHAPTER 1

How to secure the job interview.

Getting or scoring the interview for the process you choose which you need should not be rocket technology or something so difficult.Most often once in a while you could rate that interview via way of means of absolutely answering the fundamental query requested primarily based totally on easy matters which you are pre purported to recognize that you did not or that you omitted due to the fact you assumed to end that it does not rely even as it does. There are many approaches that human beings cross approximately seeking to get an interview. The strategies of attaining one range via way of means of business enterprise. It is exceptional to recognize what the business enterprises software manner is earlier than taking your first step.

Generally, whilst a business enterprise is hiring they submit an advert withinside the newspaper,radio advertisements,television advertisements or a web process bank.

How to touch them is typically blanketed withinside the advert additionally,so that you could no longer need to email your resume to a business enterprise that requests calls for you to stroll in together along with your resume and you would not need to mail a business enterprise that requests for a faxed resume from you etc,so you ignoring their unique preliminary way of contacting statistics will truly assure that you'll no longer steady that interview,the cause or reason is that you have verified and confirmed that you cannot observe easy instructions and directives.

Most of the time, you could get a process or job interview lead from a relative earlier than the process has been marketed or advertised. If that is passed off to be the case, you could both ask the relative to present the business enterprise your resume and cowl letter. If your relative doesnt definitely paintings wherein the lead got here from, you could strive calling approximately the placement and ask what the appropriate directives are.

There are 4 standard strategies of making job application,

and they encompass those unique fundamental strategies.
a.Sending a Resume:
Under this,maximum or a few corporations decide on which you mail for your resume. For this sort of technique, it'd be exceptional to encompass a cowl letter together along with your resume. The cowl is a fundamental letter that describes the placement which you are interested in and some information about your qualifications and skills. It is essentially your lead into your resume. Before you write your letter, you have to recognize whom the letter is to be addressed to, You could in no way need to start a cowl letter with Dear Sir or Madameor To whom it can also additionally Concern. It indicates that you haven't organized or readily prepared and you aren't searching out a unique role in their company or business enterprise, however this will cause you loosing the job,so you need to be prepared and ready, So not be disappointed.disrespectful in your potential business enterprise or company.So enquire very well approximately about the company or bbusiness enterprise to avoid or keep away from losing the interview.

b.Emailing Your Resume: Here,Emailing resumes is definitely turning into usual or widely a place for recruiters or job seekers to get resumes applied. Most corporations provide this technique as an opportunity to the opposite way. However, I wrote a few suggestions on the way you have to cross it or go about it.
You have to connect your resume as a phrase record,word document or PDF file. These are the maximum or most common usual formats or codecs and what maximum corporations will accept. The difficulty line has to be studied like this: William,Gerald, (clerical role). This will really make it smooth and easy for the recruiter to recognize who the email is from, and what its concerned about. It additionally assures that your e-mail will be read. Most of the time there are essentially unique strategies which an emailed resume may be addressed. Some corporations have sure difficulty line necessities so observe them. If the business enterprise you desires to seek job to needs you to stick or paste yourresume, dont send attachments due to the fact your email can be deleted instantly.

c. **Faxing Your Resume:**Faxing Your Resume, you'll want encompass or add a cover letter while you fax your resume. If you aren't using your personal fax machine, make certain to include,add or encompass your right contact informations or statistics to recognize it is coming from you for correct identification. The policies in your cover letter are similar to mailing your resume. I will offer greater information about cover letters in a while on this ebook.

d. **Walk-in Your Resume:**Under Walk-In Your Resume,For this sort of Resume application method,you will truly need to get dressed accurately and look good in appearance. You could need to get dressed much like you will for an interview. Most corporations typically ask you to walk-in Your Resume in case you are going to be operating or working directly with customers. They will ask for a walk-in Resume due to the fact they need to get a clear study of your grooming behavior properly at the moment. Sometimes, in walk-in Resume the business enterprise will need to give you a quick brief interview at the spot, to knowr if they may require a proper interview later. So be in your very exceptional,best and maximum suitable behavior. Also, walk-in Resume no longer require you to usher in a cover letter together along with your resume. Your look or your appearance is sort of kind of the cover letter. Most times, you'll be required or asked to fill out an application form too though.

Always smile and be well mannered, irrespective of who you're speaking to. That might be the distinction among getting the job interview successful.

e. **Telephoning for an interview:** Telephoning for an Interview isn't specifically not usually common anymore for corporations or companies to call you for an interview. It's typically stored for jobs that encompass income and/or jobs that aren't so without difficulty carried out for via way of means of the opposite strategies.Telephoning for an interview is a basically for job seekers who are to be mostly attending to people or the company's customers on phone calls alot. It offers them a feel for the quality and the personality of the person on the phone.When making this sort of interview request, constantly talk in a clean,suitable and bright manner. Be well mannered and organized to reply to any questions that can be requested of you. You might approach the telephone interview like this:

Hello Mr. Cole, I am Mark Richard. I am calling with the regards to your advert in the Post approximately for the clerical position. If you're requested or asked about your experience and/or past prebious work experience, be organized to reply speedy and give an explanation for how long you've been doing that previous work and give a brief description of your duties on the past job or work. Perfect manner or way to construct your resume will be added in a while on this ebook. It will come up with the perfect manner to layout your resume in order that it is observed for all the proper matters.

f.Preparing for the Interview:Once you get the notification for the interview, the following aspect that you need to do is put together for it. You can in no way over put together for an interview. The greater organized you're, the lesser tougher it is going to be to make errors. It is exceptional to put together yourself emotionally in addition to intellectually for an interview. Giving a first rate interview isn't as difficult as a few can also additionally think, however not as smooth as others do both. Here are some matters that ought to be finished so that you can put them together in your subsequent interview.

Remember, at some stage in an interview, you're a salesman. You are there to promote yourself in your potential business enterprise. You need to market or sell yourself to the maximum thrilling manner possible to your prospective employer.Awesome and amazing great guidance for the interview is your exceptional bet and it is what I have arranged and put together here for you.

g.Do Your Research:Do Your Research properly it doesnt really on how much or a lot experience or knowledgt you know in regards to the position you are trying to secure in the company,if it happens that you don't have any idea on which the company is or what they do in the company,it will be destructive,disappointing and terrible if you enter into an interview and not being capable to explain in narrative terms about what their company is all about,so there is no way you will convince them you are good and capable to be among the employees in the ccompany.

A appropriate and much less time ingesting manner to get to recognize approximately about a business enterprise is to look up their website,come to the region, ask questions and make sure fundamental information about the business enterprise from a business enterprise who's presently operating there. You can get all of the overall know-how approximately about them that manner, which include the names of key human beings or employees that work in that company and their process titles.You can as well look or sift in their pages, which include the pages that display samples in their work and/or products.

You also can look them up withinside the media documents if there are any. Read the articles approximately about them and soak in as many statistics as possible. Another aspect that could be first-rate to do is to test out is the encircling region across the business enterprise. It makes a pleasant breaker at some stage in the interview. You could make a remark about a specific monument or resting location nearby. A trickier manner to get a touch greater statistics or information approximately about the business enterprise is to name them on the smart phone and ask general and standard questios without regarding yourself as an able employee. Its a pleasant manner to get the products on upcoming promotions etc.

h.Know Your Contact: Know Your Contact
When you are called in for a job interview,make sure you inquire the appropriate person whom you will be speaking to for the job nterview, ask to whom you'll be speaking to, reason is that it will be greatly nice to greet your employer or interviewer by name at initial beginning of the job interview without being told who they are before the interview,this really proves that you definitely ready,prepared,determined for the job you are seeking for.You may also need to perform a little studies on the person who can be carrying out your interview. Learn what they do for the business enterprise and

attempt to get a few samples in their works or achievements withinside the business enterprise.

If you understand what branch that you're going to work in, you would need to get the names of your capacity colleagues and superiors prior to the job interview also.With this manner you could get a few data or information approximately about their roles withinside the corporation or company and the sorts of works that they have got done. Narrate or mention a number of the things which you learn about your capacity and potential colleagues withinside the job interview and approximately how much a good deal or how much you look forward to working with them in the future time.

i Practice Your Responses:It is first-rate, in case you are susceptible to nervousness,practice and exercise on your responses to the questions that can be asked of you,while being at home write down some possible questions which the job interviewer would ask you,meet a friend or a relative more like a brother or sister to act as the job interviewer whereby he or she will be asking you those written questions,it would prepare you,calm or reduce your nnervousness. You must exercise your wording and the tone of voice which you plan to use; Try preserving your responses as quickly as possible, however with as many elements as you could. When you are attempting to exercise session the right responses to the interviewers questions, you will additionally need to exercise the artwork of having your nerves under contro, in addition try to add yourself any other behavior or acts such expressing yourself with your hands while speaking or talking.During the time of practicing with a friend or a relative,gett his or her opinion approximately about your delivery and gestures based on how good you were during the practice. Perhaps your friend or relative can have a few first-class insights with a purpose to use in the course of the actual interview.

J. Dress the Part::Before the day of your job interview you really need to ensure that your clothes which you will wear to the job interview do not stains,wrinkls on them,wash thoroughly,iron properly,make sure you select an outfit that first-rate fits the kind of job which you are applying for. If you are going to work in an office setting , you must dress conservatively.

 Soft earth tones are first-rate for women. Try to keep away from miniskirts and shirts that display an excessive amount of skin. A first-class darkish fit is right for a male. Of direction in case you are making plans to work outdoors or an exterior job in an inventive or artistic environment, you could get dressed a little extra casually. Just be positive to keep away from sporting denim jeans, oversized clothing, and below sized clothing.Women ought to attempt to keep away from an excessive amount of makeup as well,It displays or shows the incorrect and wrong impression.Even withinside the warmer seasons, you ought to now no longer put on sandals or fitness center footwear to an interview. It sends an unprofessional message.

L.Get Organized: Make sure that every one of the things that you'll need for the job interview are organized the day before the interview.Make a checklist of the things that you'll want when you have to. You ought to constantly have a greater resume accessible at same stage in the interview. You ought to additionally carry with you a note pad to take notes at some stage in the interview if needed. (Only write down the essential matters which you assume you will want to do not forget)If you've got an enterprise card, have one accessible, it makes for clean contact later, and it additionally indicates that you are an expert or professinal and might assist the employer or the job interviewer to not forget your name.

CHAPTER 2

Ways I should act:

About the bad of effects of nervousness and being under pressure during the time of the job interview,there are many things that you can do that can take some of the pressure or nervousness off during the time of job interview. The manner in which you behave is one of the most important. Its not all in the words you say or that pop out of your mouth, however it frequently has so much to do with the mannerisms which you use.

Interviewers aren't simply thinking if you are professional sufficient or capable for the job, they may also be frequently thinking if you'll be in good fit in with your co-workers. Your personality is a huge part of your job interview and may make all of the difference. Remember this you don not have to chew gum or breath mint during your interview, you dont need to talk in slang throughout your interview either. It is unprofessional and rude.
Here are few number of the things which you have to pay attention during or throughout the job interview.

a.Show Confidence:
Never you walk into a job interview with a defeatist attitude. You can not mope or exude too or whole lot of placidity in your manner or behavior it isn't inviting, and does not give or support a good impression of someone that you want to face each day in the company.
Be certain of your talents or abilities without acting cocky or narcissistic,you will want to let your interviewer recognise and know that you are ready to perform well and greatly at your job without alienating other workers.

List your accomplishments in a pleasant way without going into an excessive amount of detail. I know this sounds repetitive. Understand that frame body language
plays a big exuding self assurance to others,siit straight,practice excellent posture, and keep your head up.

b. Keep a Positive Attitude:

You need to constantly smile and hold a high-quality outlook in the course of your interview. If what you are
listening to is something that doesnt sound good to you, dont frown and look disgruntled, simply keep a slight mild smile on your face till it's time for you to mention or say something. Then meet your interviewer together with your questions or issues whilst the time is appropriate.

c.Maintain Eye Contact:

Know this,it's Important,always keep or maintain eye contact with your interviewer especially when he is speaking to you or when you are speaking back to the interviewer. If you're looking across the room on the gadgets at the Interviewer's desk, you may seem uninterested or you will appear or look as a shy type of person or you are a type of person that can't listen attentively.

d.Body Language:

Weve touched this a bit but however you need to notice and observe some of the mistakes or errors that many human beings make when they're speaking to others. Ive indexed few numbers of things which you need to keep away whilst sitting infront an interview.

.Prevent fidgeting at the same time when speaking with your interviewer. It shows lack of self confidence.

.Avoid talking at the same time as the usage of overly expressive hand gestures. It is distracting.

.Avoid biting your lips in sentences. It shows the Impression that that you are making things up.

.Never take a seat down together with your palms crossed as it makes you seem stand-offish.

.Never shrug your shoulders when asked a question which you are uncertain of. Take a second to consider your response. Shrugging your shoulders offers the impact that you dont know the answer.

.Never answer with nods and head shakes. Use your phrases or words to reply to questions.

.Get enough sleep the night before the interview. You dont need to yawn in front of the interviewer. He will assume that you are expressing boredom.

e.Your First Impression matters:

Always remember that first impressions matters alot, it may be a difficult thing to get beyond or get past first impression in any situation. During an interview you need to offer the excellent first impact or impression that you could. There are many small things that you could do to guarantee that you provide the excellent impact possible. They are as follows:

.You can not be way too well polite to the individual that directs to your waiting area when waiting to be interviewed.A small gesture like,asking how they are doing can work wonders for you when you leave the building later.

.While ready to be interviewed, sit well trained and mannered and behave as if everyone passing you by is your potential interviewer.Never act impatient tired or bored,it sends wrong message,some job interviewer will intentionally keep you waiting to see how will behave and handle yourself.

.Greet your interviewer with firm handshake and a smile. Keep standing until your interviewer asks you to be seated. It is virtually well mannered and indicates right etiquette.

. Again, get dressed in according to the kind of job you are applying for. Show yourself to be properly organized, through having all things needed for the interview.

.While waiting do not eat or drink anything.

. Dont chat on your phone even as you are wsiting for your interviewer. It makes you appear distracted not focused.

f.Your Resume:
This might also additionally appear like an unimportant issue
all through an interview, however that is the only purpose
why you might also additionally get that interview so that you
ought to be organized with a nicely written resume.
You ought to tailor your resume to spotlight the
qualifications, work experience and any education which
youve had that quality represents the sort of work you're
making use of for. You ought to additionally add or include
every other work you might have had in addition to any
accomplishments which you have made in your field.

You also need to dress up your resume to allow it to stand
out a bit. A great border is an elegant manner to make your
resume stand out without being a distraction to the records
inside it.Of course there are additionally pretty some things
that recruiters hate to see on resumes as well. Many human
beings do not think that recruiters really go through all of the
way through a resume, however they surely do.
Recruiters have ceetain pet peeves in relation to studying a
resume. In this book Ive added a list of the peeves which you
ought to keep away from whent putting your resume
together.

These are the things that recruiters hate to see:

a.Not showing or including essential and vital information on
a resume is disastrous. A recruiter desires to see all your
 essential records and documents without having to look for
 it.

b.Major gaps in your employment records leaves a recruiter
wondering about your work ethics. Be prepared to answer
questions when you have such gaps in yours.

c.Summaries which can be tough to observe aAnd
apprehend are traumatic to recruiters. Keep your precisely
smooth and brief.

d.Use easy and simple fonts. Fancy fonts and color aren't
eye catching as you think,the most important thing is that
your resume must be neat,well typed and also having what

they really desire from you.

e.Avoid writing your resume as a story or in the first or third person, It is really irritating for a recruiter, and is derived off as boastful, arrogant and egotistical.

f.Pictures or graphics on a resume are distracting to a recruiter. Things like that will likely get your resume tossed out without a glance.

g.Needlessly including goals and introductions for your resume bores recruiters,they
know what your goal is, and your resume isn't supposed to be a novel.

h. Lying or placing deceptive statistics or information on your resume is a primary anf major no-no. There are usually methods for a recruiter to test or check up on what many do, so dont lie. Getting caught in a lie on a resume simply shows that you cant be trusted.

I.Adding useless or unnecessary information on a resume like your hobbies is absolutely useless. You have to keep that section to explain any accomplishments which you have made in your field.

j.Sending a resume that doesnt match the sort of job which you are applying for is extraordinarily irritating to a recruiter because you are wasting their time.

k. Using overly lengthy paragraphs in a resume gets yours tossed aside. It is more difficult for the recruiter to read and makes the task take too long.

l. Resumes which might be greater or more than two pages will not be fully ready by the recruiter. Thats simply.

m. Dating the information on your work records in the incorrect order makes your resume more difficult to follow. (Work records have to be indexed with maximum cutting-edge jobs on the top).

n. Resumes which have an excessive amount of details when talking about your previous duties are a waste of your time. Duties are normally simply sifted through. They are hardly given very much attention, simply just enough to show or give the recruiter a concept of what you've got executed or done in the past.

o. Spelling and grammatical mistakes simply proves that you aren't very eager for details.

CHAPTER 3

The Dos and Don'ts

There are very few things which you truly should not have to do and to do during an interview encounter that appears to make the complete factor lots less complicated for each of you and the questioner. I listed them here in this book below.

Dos

a. Arrive on time, or better yet arrive 10mins early.

b.   Refer to the interviewer by name.

c. Smile and use a firm handshake.

d. be alert and act interested throughout the whole job interview.

c. Maintain eye contact at all times.

d. Make all comments in a positve manner.

e . Speak clearly,firmly,and with authority.

f. Except any refreshment offered to you.

g. Promote your strengths.

Don'ts

a. Don't be overly aggressive pr egotistical.

b. Don't spend too much time talking about money better still don't focus on my but focus specifically on how best you will be for the company,because the interviewer will conclude that all you care about is money.

c. Don't act uninterested in the company or the job.

d. Don't speak badly about past colleagues or employers.

e. Don't answer with only yes or no.

f.. Don't excuse your bad points about work history.

g. Don't excuse yourself halfway through the job interview even if you have to use the bathroom that's why you are told or adviced to make sure to use the bathroom earlier before the interview starts.

Your cover letter

Creating the perfect cover letter doesn't have to be difficult. Cover letters are usually short and to the point. You should address your cover page to a specific person. You should never address your cover letter "To Whom It May Concern"or "Dear

 Sir/Madam."It is unprofessional and shows no genuine interest in the company or the job.
The cover letter is the sole purpose for looking at the resume.If it is written badly,the resume might not get a once over.The cover letter should begin with a basic greeting and the position that you are applying for.It should not be more than 2 lines long.The second paragraph should be a brief description of your qualifications and why you applied to work for them. The closing should announce an interest in hearing from them soon,and a thank you for their time.

Here is a sample of a successful cover letter.

****

****

June 25, 2022
In regards to: The clerical position that is available.
Mr. William
4363 Richard St.
Richard City,FA
4215
Attention: Mr. Mark William
Dear Mr. William
This letter is in regards to the clerical position that is recently available in your company.As my enclosed resume will show you,I have three years experience as a clerk. During my career I have successfully integrated a new filling system for my previous employer, Gerald telecommunication firm that increased their productivity by 43%. That filling system is still in use there now, and has been integrated into two other companies.
I thank you for your time in reading this letter. I hope to hear from you once you have had time to read my resume.
Respectfully,
Your name
Enclosure (1)

The restaurant interview

Sometimes recruiters will ask you to conduct your interview at some point during lunch or dinner. It makes a greater comfortable setting for the recruiter, however you need to recollect or remember that it's still an interview, and your

conduct or behavior should be according to that.
During this form of interview, you need to look at it as a relaxing way for you to talk about and sell yourself to the recruiter. Making a little bit of small talk is expected. Do not carry up the subject of the interview till the interviewer does. He/she would possibly need to get to understand you a piece first.
Remember to speak approximately about yourself, however do not get too personal. There also are simple points of etiquette and common sense rules that you follow as well.They are as follows:

a.Remember your simple basic table manners, like putting your elbows at the desk etc.

b. Always fold your serviette or napkin on your lap before eating.

c. Do not order the most messy or sloppy foods. That consists of finger foods like ribs, and extremely massive sandwiches. Avoid pastas with thick sauces, and French fries.

c.Do now not order the most highly-priced or expensive item on the menu either.

d. Avoid alcoholic liquids if you can.

e.When you rise up to use the restroom, place your napkin on your chair or on the arm of your chair.

f.Common sense; dont smack your lips or speak with your mouth full.

g. Always excuse yourself in case you plan to depart the desk for any reason.

h. Do not have your mobile pone turned on.
Continue to speak officially to your interviewer until asked not to.After your interview is over, be certain to thank the recruiter for the meal and their time. Offer a corporate firm handshake, and ask when you should expect to hear from

them It shows self belief,confidence and a a continued interest in the job. Send a thanks card that same day.

Closing the interview

Once you've run the bases of the interview, it's still critically Important that you end the interview well,the difficult part is over and now all that remains is for you to close out the interview in same winning attitude.You have to wait till your interviewer stands up or requests that you do too,give your closing greeting,thank the interviewer for making out time to see you,offer another firm handshake and ask when you might expect to hear from them about their decision.

Extra Tips

Additionlally with all the statistics and informations that was given on this manual book,you would have assume or think that you have learned everything that there is there to know about acing an interview however there are still a few extra tips that you should know and a few more,below are few tips or hints that you should know more about.

1. You will have to market your capabilities,skills and associated experiencel in the field which you are applying for,try and be sure to do it in a manner that is positive and not tricky or cocky.

2 It is also a good to research about the company before your interview to know exactly where you would fit,it allows or makes the employer that you're serious and interested in the job and that you really want to a part of the company too.

3. You should also come with the lists of questions with you in a folder with the company's name on it so that you don't forget them,also you have to keep the extra remaining resume there.

4. You need to explain your weaknesses as strengths. For example, pronouncing that you are overenthusiastic, approximately performing at your best.

5. Whenever interviewers ask you what your biggest fault
might be, you have to
Select a fault that is simply a good thing. Try saying I dont
tackle tasks that I
cant provide 110% on.
6. Let your interviewer deliver up the subject of income first.
7. Dont volunteer your non-public or personal opinions to
your interviewer about any subject unless you are asked.
8. Try to set up or establish a good with your interviewer,be
professional and be real.

Common Interview Questions

Every interview composes of the interviewer asking you a
wonderful deal of questions. Many of these are standard
questions that each interviewer asks. Ive listed the most
questions that you will come across during an interview to
help you get a handle on them before you go to job
interview,it's usually necessary and important to be prepared
ahead of the job interview
By reading all these important questions that interviewers
ask,you will have an ahead knowledge and most opportunity
to win the job interview competition.Additional you also have
time to prepare your answers ahead of the job interview so
that you don't get stumped.So here is your key to acing a job
interview.
1. Tell me something about yourself. Remember, say
something positive.
2. How do manage or handle stressful situations?
3. How do you cope or deal with complaints and stress?
4. What is your definition of success?
5.Why do you think that you would fit in with this
company?(Here is where what you researched comes in
handy)
6. Have you ever been fired, and why?
7. Where do you see yourself in five years?
8. Do you prefer to work on your ownl or as a team?
9. Why are you interested in working for this company?
10. How do you deal with or handle a different of opinion
together with your colleagues or superiors?
11. Why do i need to hire you?

CHAPTER 4

Common Questions while applying for your first Job after College Graduation.

1.Briefly tell me what your most rewarding college experience was?
2. What extracurricular sports or activities did you take part in?
3. What have you ever discovered in university that applies immediately to this job?
4. How have you ever prepared yourself for the transition from university to the
workplace?
5. Are you going to graduate school? If so, do you propose or plan to retain worng as
well?
6. How do you propose to manage graduate school and working?
7. Did you get any hands on experience in School?
8. How do you feel that university has organized and prepared you for this job?
9. Have you ever had or done an internship that helped to put together or prepare you for this kind of work?
10. What do you think is the best ana pleasant asset that you can bring or render o the company?

Questions that you should ask your interviewer

Likewise and just like you'll be fielding questions from your interviewer, it's far pleasant to also ask few of your own very important intelligent neccessary questions too,it shows that you are genuinly intelligent,smart and also mostly interested in working in the company.

Below are few questions which you should ask your prospective interviewer
1. Why is that this position is available right now?
2. How many times has this postion been filled in the past five years?
3.What should the new employee do that is different from the last employee that has this position?

4. What would you mostly like to see done in the next 6 months?
5. What are the maximum hard issues that this jobs entails?
6. How much freedom do I actually have in he decision making process?
7. What are my alternatives for advancement?
8. How has this company succeeded withinside the past?
9. What modifications do you envision in future for this corporation?
10. What do you think constitutes success on this task?

Questions that employers cannot ask

Just like there are various questions that an interviewer can ask, there are various that he cannot ask. Some questions are illegal to ask. Many human beings dont understand that there are off limit questions for employers. That is why I felt that it has to be critically added here in this book.
When or if you do encounter some of the questions, there are processes that you can choose to answer them. Since some human beings may probably answer them, it's far good to understand that you dont ought to answer those varieties of questions. You can honestly ask how those questions pertain to the work or job that are youre be rendering. Here is a list of the questions that
are illegal for an interviewer to ask.
1. Questions about your age are not allowed during an interview because it should not be a factor upon hiring or employing you.

2. Questions about your marital status are beside inappropriater and may easily mistaken for sexual harassment. This question moreover aapplies to any personal questions that are been asked,you can easily and gently reply how does it pertain in employing and if the interviewer or the employer then explains why it's required to be answered then you can answer it in a way that would be appropriate.
3. Questions about your non-public health are also off limits,but sometimes its required to know if the company is safe from you so you would know how to go about it that's how you personally want to address the question or how

best you would want to answer it.
4. Questions about your ethnicity should not to be asked during an interviewer or answered by the person being given the interview.
5. Your sexual preference cannot be factor il in your opportunities of being hired either.
6. Whether or not you have disabilities is a question that should not be asked either.
7. Your arrest file is records that don't ought to be answered back. All an interviewer can ask you if you have ever been convicted of a crime, they cannot ask you what for or how many times.
8. Basically, personal information can't be requested or asked by an interviewer,it is illegal and you do not have to answer.with the aid of using an interviewer.

The Post Interview Follow-up

Now that the interview is over, the difficult work is over, however you still have follow up the interview later. Sending a thank you note is the best manner to start. The thanks letter ought to be written together along with your thank you for his or her time and attention in seeing you.

If you havent heard from the company or from the employer within a week, you have to call the office to ask if they have reached a decision yet.This not being pushy,it shows your enthusiasm and persistence,within a week may be early to call so it wouldn't sound as if you are pushy,wait up to a month,if they have not reached a decision yet,ask when you might expect to hear from them.If they don't give an answer try again in next a week time and so on but if they have your contact number or email it's left for them to get back to you only if you are given the job or employed.

What Employers are looking for

When an enterprise or a company makes a decision to conduct an interview with you, there are positive thimgs that they're seeking out from you. Naturally, you're probably to cognizance on these things in the course of an interview, however you ought to recollect all the pointers on this guide due to the fact following those
pointers or tips are what will make the employers see all of these things in you.

Since everyone desires to have a leg up in when it comes to a job nterview, it naturally regarded to be suitable to let you in on what the employers are comparing you with in the course of an interview. So right below here is that list.

1.Your Enthusiasm:
Employers need to know that you are willing, inclined and keen to be a part of their corporation or company. Being absolutely stocked with understanding knowledge the corporation is a positive hearthplace manner to show your enthusiasm.

2. Your capabilities to talk clearly: If it happened that you meet an interview mumbling and speaking slang,a prospective interviewer or employer will not see you as a professional.

3. Showing your teamwork skills: you should show an example of your ability work as during your iinterview.

4. Leadership skills: You need to display your leadership abilities by approaching your interview with an offensive rain of thought.

5.Problem fixing capability: Employers desires to recognise that you may deal with yourself while a problem arrives.

6.Work related experience: You sincerely need to show that you have some experience in the field already, in order that the company s aware that you will not be overwhelmed.

7.Community involvement: Employers love to see that you have accomplished volunteer work,It indicates that you take delight in your community, and a willingness to be a team player.

8.Company knowledge: Additional this stipulates that employers want to see that you have researched about their company,it reveals that your interest in working for them in sincere.

9.Flexibility: Employers need to recognise that you are

capable of going with the flow. It proves that they are able to rely on you later.

10.Ambition and Motivation: Ambitious human beings are usually motivated sufficiently enough to make extraordinary upgrades or improvements in the agency or company as they may are working their up to the ladder.Here ambition typically means more money for the company.

11.People skills: They want to recognise that you wont ruffle any feathers while you are hired.

12.Professional appearance: No one desires a slob operating their office,so always certain,serious,determines and positive to appear professionally.

13.Ability to multitask: This is to be a completely important ability in the office. You will be required to multitask if you are not a multitask kind of person employers need to know that you can do that without freaking out on them.

14.Computer ease: Nowadays, pretty much every company or organisation in the world is running on computers. The capability to work with a computer at least minimal amount of ease is so important. Its so common and important to keep a leg up on the common Softwares like MS Office,Quark Express, and Linux Quarkxpress, and Linux.

15.Reliability:: Employers need reliable and dependable humans to work for them. Your capacity to reach or arrive on time is a great area to begin when trying to show or prove that have this reliable quality.

Employer Evaluations

Employers are usually tracking,monitoring and comparing you on 3 ability units during job interview. . Those 3 ability units can effortlessly be broken down into the following sections below:

1.Content Skills: These are the talents or skills which are immediately associated with performing a specific job in your profession.You get these skills by learning your your craft in an accredited school through specialized training,work experience,attaining a degree, and internships.This proves or displays that an employer that you are have acquired all of the required knowledge that you need to perform your job efficiently.

And if you don't have this sort of ability you can simply express that you are looking into specialized training,and would be willing to start.It may not be exactly what the employer is looking for,but it shows that you display initiative.

2. Functional Skills: Functinal skills are the talents,skills or ability that replicate or reflects capacity to do work with others, and the way you incorporate
data. This is wherein a company or employer makes a decision whether you are or you are not team player.r. You can show this talent or skill through showing your past employment record and accomplishments that are directly job related.
Generally an enterprise or company gets a concept or idea of your cap potential to work with others relying on your motives for leaving previous jobs, whether or not you were fired before and so on. And if you have been fired before,don't lie about it,and do not act bitter about it when discussing the reason,when you lie it will affect you in the end because these companies have ways of finding out the truth.Be forth coming and sincere.Show and express it was a learning experience for you and tell them what you learned from it.It reflects well on your temperament.

3.Adaptive Skils: Adaptive Skills displays or reveals your character,your personality and temperament. It additionally covers yourself control capabilities and management skills. During your interview, the enterprise or company can be comparing you for your preferred cap potential to get at the side of him/her. Your preferred character trends are monitored throughout this time.
When confronted with a hard question, you no longer need to get protective or angry. Just take some seconds to consider what you have to say instead of say something you will regret. If you must; sincerely provide an explanation for which you are a bit apprehensive so you should buy some more seconds to answer.

You need to seem at ease, (or as a lot in order you can) throughout your interview. You need the enterprise or company to assume that you anticipated everything that he or she is going to say.even if you are terrified at your replies and finally do not let them know that you sweat.All these are what and what you ought to know to win a job competition.

Summary

By this moment, you've discovered and learned everything or the most important things that you would need to know before you go in for a job interview. Here in this book manual you have acquired the necessary required skills needed to get and ace any job interview that you would go on.You have made the accurate move in choosing this book manual as your guide.As promised,you are going to approach your next job interview with a leg up on the competition.By now you have been able to learn how to:

1.Get the job interview of your choice or dream.
2. How to prepare for the job interview.
3.The best way to behave and during job interview.
4. How to make a great great first impression.
5. How to build a best great resume for your dream job.
6. How to create a winning cover page.
7. What to do during a restaurant interview.
8. How to dress for success.
9. How to close an interview.
10. What kinds of questions that you will be asked in a job interview.
11. What questions that you should asked during job interview.
12. What questions that you can not ask during the job interview.
13. How to follow up on your Interview.
14. What employers are directly looking for from you.

So by now you have acquired and learned everything that you need to know about winning and getting the job you dream about from this book manual guide,and a little more than that. You have increased your chance of getting that your dream job by 100% or 98% . If you are due to have a job interview, you now already learned how to ace the job interview just by reading this manual,so read it more and more whenever you have a job interview to attend to.Good luck.

ABOUT THE AUTHOR

Mac Nekzy is from US, he studied in US.